NANCY JO CULLEN

# NOTHING WILL SAVE YOUR LIFE

POEMS

# OTHER TITLES

*by Nancy Jo Cullen*

**POETRY**

*Pearl*
*Science Fiction Saint*
*untitled child*

**FICTION**

*Canary*
*The Western Alienation Merit Badge*

POEMS

# NOTHING WILL
# SAVE YOUR LIFE

BY NANCY JO CULLEN

A Buckrider Book

Published by Buckrider Books
an imprint of Wolsak and Wynn Publishers
280 James Street North
Hamilton, ON L8R2L3
www.wolsakandwynn.ca

Editor: Paul Vermeersch | Copy editor: Ashley Hisson
Cover and interior design: Kilby Smith-McGregor
Cover image: iStock by Getty Images
Author photograph: Kristen Ritchie
Typeset in Freight Text Pro and Balboa Plus
Printed by Coach House Printing Company, Toronto, Canada

10 9 8 7 6 5 4 3 2 1

 Canada Council    Conseil des Arts        Canadä
for the Arts      du Canada

The publisher gratefully acknowledges the support of the Ontario Arts Council, the Canada Council for the Arts and the Government of Canada.

**Library and Archives Canada Cataloguing in Publication**

Title: Nothing will save your life : poems / Nancy Jo Cullen.
Names: Cullen, Nancy Jo, author.
Identifiers: Canadiana 20220159343 | ISBN 9781989496503 (softcover)
Classification: LCC PS8555.U473 N68 2022 | DDC C811/.54—dc23

*For Helen*

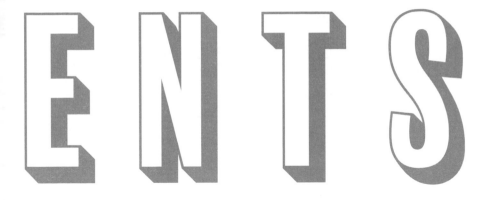

ONE

# Ghosts

I think it's fair to say that even before her death our mother gave up the ghost
her body troubled by the clogged arteries of her mind
by her arch sadness and by her affection for sugar.

She dragged us through our childhoods
angry and anxious.
Her epic silences –

On the plane to our brother's funeral she forgot she was afraid to fly,
forgot our brother was dead. To think he endured the mishap of his birth
and paper routes only to find himself in that predeceasing position.

But first, he gave up his tender shadows;
he gave up drink, then the tip of his baby finger to the oil rig
and then cigarettes – too late, I fear.

For a moment our mother remembered who was lost
and grief shuffled out of her throat
on the icy day our brother's coffin was lowered into the ground.

Later we tucked our mother into bed. We left her teeth in a cup. We
poured wine and lit a smoke. Who knows what we talked about,
our brother's giggle or the furious chain that tore off his finger?

# *TBH*

1.

Teenagers are pulling their braces off with their bare hands
Illuminating the unlit valley of adolescence with their exposed midriffs
Subjecting mothers to the Sacrament of Contempt
Mothers are crying into their cold-pressed, non-GMO organic juice
The mothers of the mothers have had too much sun
Fragile little snowbirds, their bones are disintegrating
Such extremely low thresholds for enduring discomfort
They can't even; they just can't
Nobody asks to be born
Not to mention all that plastic accumulating in the landfill
When they said crisis response planning they meant anti-wrinkle cream
Accustom yourself to plaintive disregard
Nobody asks to be a YouTube instructional video gone wrong
Not to mention all that human trash accumulating in the belly of the whale

2.

Not to mention all that human trash accumulating in the belly of the whale
Nor the invisible doctrine of the invisible hand and its invisible backers
Nor the offshore holdings of the Father and the Son & Sons
Currently in a loss position for tax purposes
Devastating, that feeling we failed ourselves in the land of opportunity
The uncertain sickly appetite to please[1]
Think of something meaningful to say to the kids:
TBH, freedom for the pike is death for the minnows
The body keeps the score, our long history of anxiety
In the province of ongoing extirpation
Still, there is the miracle of the softening mud and dog shit, flagrant
Uproar of the hermit thrush, the white-throated sparrow
The brown creeper, the Earth turning again toward warm days
The wonder of the Body, TBH, is Its capacity for punishment

---

1    William Shakespeare, Sonnet 147.

3.

The wonder of the body, TBH, is its capacity for punishment
We told our daughters, Do not walk through that park; we said
You are a public space & it will not soon end
You are open for business 24-7, sweetheart
That age-old Madonna–"she has no respect for herself" divide
The need to think critically about a safe space
Say yes, say yes to the dress; say no
Say sorry, say my fault; say please
Anyway, what she can or can't eat is practically all she will think
About, a nuanced dance of tactics and selection
And the Instagram effect now that nature isn't natural
Confession of our faults is the next thing to innocence
Follow the thought of envy
The rich live, the rich live longer everywhere

4.

The rich live, the rich live longer everywhere
The rich think, the rich think about think pieces
By think piece they mean hip & knee replacement surgery
By hip & knee replacement surgery they mean inheritance
By inheritance they mean embrace sincerity
By embrace sincerity they mean deposit the proceeds of social conditioning
They mean to say, efficiency algorithms are their jam
They mean welcome to the so-called sharing economy
We push the walk button; we push the walk button again
We push the walk button again; we are on fire at the intersection
Our bones consumed in the noise, the weather
Some girls *imagine* they feel worse than they do
They get into a dither just by thinking too much about themselves[2]

---

2    *You're a Young Lady Now* (Neenah, WI: Kimberly-Clark, 1961).

5.

They get into a dither just by thinking too much about themselves
Their informational appliances are always at their fingertips
Their fingertips are always on the receiving end
Of the global supply chain, always on the receiving end
Of standout online dating profile photos
Always on the receiving end of palatable versions of
Demographically segmented market variables
Always on the receiving end of the body in trouble
Brought on by an insufficiency of imagination & upcycled
Dresses; brought on by the absence of absence
And the plastic particulate matter of a bifurcated heart
Your continued participation serves as express consent
Bring your noise-cancelling headphones
The Lord helps those who help themselves

6.

Because the Lord helps those who help themselves
Because all the cats want to dance with the natural mutation
Because of the heat-trapping nature of sweet little sixteen
Because of the inability to recall the sequence of traumatic events
Because of the tendency of attention to be affected by recurring thoughts
Because of record-breaking high temperatures
Because of mitigation and adaptation
Because of benzodiazepine
Because of twenty-one words used to describe only women
Because of sharks, dogs, mountains, elevators and mosquitoes
Because of blacklegged ticks and American presidential elections
Because of selective serotonin reuptake inhibitors
Because of smiley face emoticons
Because of clinical levels of acquisitiveness

7.

Because of clinical levels of acquisitiveness
And all the angels & saints in their "spiritual gangster" T-shirts
All the latest patrons of leisure, style and taste
All the latest patrons of teenaged girls, angular and hungry
Feeling their supreme moment of destiny
Teenaged girls waiting to spring into time
And by time they mean take their husband's name
And by all the angels & saints they mean reality TV stars
They mean they have no sense of their overdetermined circumstances
This poem is bitter; this poem has gone to fat
This poem is crushing the dreams of teenaged girls
It tells them they are still unloved
But those girls are laughing and this poem is an old bitch
And teenagers are pulling their braces off with their bare hands

# Current Mood

A mountain (the way we think of a mountain)
Assuming we think of the mountain as mean
A sudden, damaging turn in doctrine
The collision of songbird with windscreen
Immanent or occurring thunderstorms
A dog, alone and shaking in the dark
The feeling will pass, the feeling that warns
The dog, alone and shaking in the dark
So by the time we name it, it has gone
That madness has left the brain's stadium
My mood, a runaway phenomenon
A vestige of my old Catholicism
A remembrance of everything I lack
A tribute to what God might just take back

# Due

Perhaps it's the flu or, perhaps, fury
& the news is too fast for my feelings
in this political economy
where the profit wants what the profit wants.
I'm trying to lighten up, to sparkle
but my children are in their own cities
& my dog, mysteriously failing,
now sleeps under the stove. I'm paralyzed.

*In a small town fraught with sins and secrets,*[3]
A day of concern for your waitress please
& the Maker you made in your own image.
Waiting on the trickle-down effect here
wearied by the Patriarchy's patriarchs
I am trying not to hate this world –

---

3    Promo bumpf from Netflix's *Dark*.

# Bubble

Everything we want is on our timeline
& all our fifty thousand thoughts per day
are a limbic reactivity feed
so the formation of our memories
(and also our higher mental functions)
spring from too many places of disease
in the 1980s' sense of the word,
when we shouted: *yes means yes & no means no*
*dis/ease*, 'cause we continue to reinvent
the fucking wheel & still call it progress,
like how we are starring in a shit show
of our own making proves we are still just sad
children of the children who were still sad
in this new winter of our discontent.

## *Heaven*

My folks took me to Mass that I might adore
Jesus & fear God and by my fear comply,
bear patiently each day's disappointments
and calmly await my certain demise,
for even before my use of reason
sin was in my soul. No consolation
in my corporeal form & no joy
only terrible anticipation.
This short explanation of my youthful
dread reminds me of a joke I forget
and that our memories are so much false
belief about what we want to believe;
like we are deserving of our bounty,
that everything happens for a reason.

## Humans on Mars

And now, the hottest month yet recorded
While fire creates its own wind & takes flight
And the eternal shore waits, endangered
And (again) we have sinned through our own fault.
My darling gluttons, it is our misfortune
To find theory simpler than its practice
& our aggregate Gods an affliction
In the spectacular shadow of business.
Our kids have become students of commerce
They're rolling out affordable flights to Mars
Such adorable little emigrants
We'll email our children in outer space
Then four to thirty minutes later they'll read,
*And now, the hottest month yet recorded.*

## Something to Cry About

Picture my mother in 1968 watching the television news
perhaps that year she put her faith in God, or perhaps in Valium.
Now I am adrift in new storms and catastrophes, and

in the presence of my anxieties, my mother is not wholly dead.
Perhaps she put her faith in God, or perhaps in Valium
that year of assassinations and the generation gap.

I hear her in my head; she is saying something about the mystery of faith.
Maybe she said, Do you want me to give you something to cry about?
It was probably ordinary pities and fears that consumed my mother

in that year of assassinations and the generation gap.
She suffered from nerves; she went to her doctor, and she went to confession.
I suppose that, like my mother, I worry too much.

That is not a blaming statement. I think of her in 1968
watching the television news, and faithless creature that I've become,
I still hear her in my head: Do I want her to give me something to cry about?

# Nothing Beside Remains

*Dialogue with it is impossible. For us to live and die properly, things have to be named properly. Let us reclaim our words.*

– John Berger, "Where Are We?"

Still the mud unburies its secrets,
while every Tom, Dick and King of Kings races to erect
his sprawling monument to profit perched atop
narrow, trash-strewn streets brimming with noise and poverty[4]
proving that one man's treasure was first another man's trash.
That empires have fallen is not apocryphal.
Look, children have Instagrammed themselves with the poor head of the
colossus.
Ever have we elevated greed above the plume thistle
the river, the winter robin. The civility of empire is a fable.
Dialogue with it is impossible.

But before we were the lost, we were the living things,
forgettable children of foot soldiers and washerwomen,
partisan little attendants with unbalanced hearts
& blameworthiness as our daily portion in the electoral district
of tears, waiting to shuffle into the sweet by and by,
to leave behind our toil for that beautiful shore
and the wind, unexpected and familiar,
and the store of unconscious fear memories
we believed we needed to believe
for us to live – and die – properly.

---

4    Declan Walsh, "Statue Being Pulled from a Gritty Patch of Cairo Could Be of
     Ramses," *New York Times*, March 10, 2017.

Now we line up in cars at the drive-thru as we double-double down,
while our ahistorical children play under the backyard tree
(those darling digital citizens of our wombs).
Meanwhile, broadcast across glass, phosphor, cerium, plastics, copper,
tin, zinc, silicon, gold & chromium: The spectacle of human migration,
displacement as entertainment industry,
kitten videos as news of the day,
plus the variation, mutation, competition & inheritance of memes
despair has become –
"things have to be named properly."

Until drop by drop, the sorrowful mysteries, the escalations,
the grace. What has absence of worry to do with beauty,
little bird? We reside in the body; we exist on the body
for these tender minutes in our orbital tours.
Kings and serfs and shoppers all
lift our confirmation biases heavenwards.
The mud is surrendering its cargo; the poor children of Instagram
are trending on this living system of interdependent
living systems, hosanna, hosanna –
Let us reclaim our words.

# Current Mood

You and your blankety-blank left-leaning bender –

It's easier for a camel to pass through the eye of a needle than that tawdry science at the back of your mind. A tiny superego represents your ego & all the beautiful, unrealized plans you do not. You do not deserve to be forgiven. You do not deserve the Kingdom, the security of the manicured lawn, the shade tree, your mother sipping a gin & tonic on the porch. Your mother sitting on the porch of a house she never owned. No one is saved by the faith of others. No one is saved by taking shorter showers. You know what you don't even know you know, like how when your mother died she didn't even know your name.

# Non Sequitur

I'm studying unease with the natural world – western blacklegged
tick, Rocky Mountain wood tick, deer tick. All shifty little nightmares.

Speaking of man's fall, I am a fan of apples, abundant & waxy world travellers,
dropped from tree to produce departments at $2.49/lb.

I wouldn't say I'm ashamed of my nakedness, of my careworn body. I
can still bite into the fruit of good & evil. Hey, man, I can still get it up.

But I'm as clear as I've ever been about love, whatever the fuck love is, while
worry creeps along my body in search of a tender piece.

I have no idea what's coming next. Sometimes I laugh; sometimes I just go
bonkers. I do not have the success habit, that one thing I can do –

Trouble likes to nestle behind ears & under armpits. And in our groins, where,
the story goes, all sin originated. Oh, wicked boxes of delight.

FYI, vanilla is a difficult food – fruit of the hand pollinated, hermaphroditic
orchid. But really, shouldn't we all reach into our beloveds just so?

I don't want your Father's forgiveness. I have the gift of her pocket knife. I
want her, & our bodies rolling away from one another in the summer heat.

# Glorious Bitches

Once, your boyfriend squeezed into our living room through the window
we left open just wide enough for the cat
Thirty-five years later he rings into this present moment, unbidden
though we're not on mushrooms
and *Being There* is not on the late movie
and we have free cross-country calling
and we can no longer party like we used to,
and I've put in my hearing aids, so the tone of your beloved voice is clear

It seems impossible that we are no longer those young women
with a taste for the extreme
as if pain was truer than peace
and only knuckleheads settled for the quiet life
lol, right?

Those losses we collected like thrift-store cowboy boots
until we finally submitted to the daydream of motherhood
Such a wicked surprise, that monotony
how suddenly we were so fucking boring
so tired, so disappointed, so undesirable, so undesiring
We are always returned to our miscalculations

And now your fragile old boyfriend is clawing back through time
inserting himself through the looping monster of the Internet
literally crazy as a loon as our mothers would have said
his boundaries as shite as ever
But for a moment we become glorious bitches
and we laugh at the damages, his and ours
What were we ever thinking?

Then you give me a brief rundown on sativa and indica
because don't we deserve some relief?
Didn't we raise our children
– all the while our hearts pounding in our throats
those delicate disasters
we cannot shrug off –
only to find we have failed as bigly as our own mothers
and our ex-lovers are old or dead or mad

## Current Mood

If our work is concerned with universals
our bottom lines belong to daddy

He's got the whole world in his hands
and (within an allowable variation)
we're locked in by POV and marriageability

Do we look fat in this thinking?

## Nothing Will Save Your Life

Fifty percent of the Beatles are dead.
Not even poetry will save my life
& its relentless mix of joy and dread
epitomized by my days playing wife.
But anyway, half the Beatles are dead
& I remember my sisters dancing
with their own reflections in the darkened
living room window; yeah, yeah, yeah –
Now, on the darkest, longest night ever
while my dog is snoring on her pillow
(surely five hundred years is forever)
I pull the curtain across the window
& shut out the dark; shut out the longest night.
I've lost the only faith I ever had.

Well, I lost the one faith I thought I had.
But first, I was a child of devotion.
I wanted to be a saint, to be loved
like the Beatles, like Mother Teresa
who, I've heard, was as mean as a nun.
I believed that my sin was egregious
& my reward in heaven uncertain
– I mean, Jesus.
So then, when my sister plucked my brows,
each yank was a provocation; each yank
a penance. We're born to suffer anyhow
& I was tormented by my teenaged rank.
That was the year I was ugly and hopeless;
that first year of my dad's diagnosis.

That was the year of my dad's diagnosis
& all those girls who loved Peter Frampton
with his dreamy hair curled round his shoulders.
We thought our lives would wondrously open.
It was a full nine minutes to midnight
in 1976 and we got high
on homemade apricot wine & weak pot.
The year my dad learned that his end was nigh
I read through my brother-in-law's porno
stash where all hot chicks waited on all dull
men; hard-nippled, wet-pussied, painted-on
shirt ladies hot & horny as all hell
They didn't fear eternal damnation.
Call that my sexual awakening.

Call that my sexual awakening.
Or call it my dream of crashing airplanes,
of unrealistic goals & fear of dying,
to which I'd add my dreams of pulling teeth.
(Those teeth linked to every anxiety.)
Not even Peter Frampton could save me
from the news of my dad's fatal disease;
the dread of that impending disaster.
But I digress from the topic of porn
as instruction in my ineptitudes.
My wish to be desirable outdone
by a boy's disappointing advances.
My so-called awakening –
a private estrangement from my desire.

All estranged from my desire. My desire
lifted on gusts above the trees, detached
from this place of my body; a cipher.
Not to suggest I was broken hearted.
Not to suggest I wasn't. When my mom
walked down the aisle she prayed for no regrets,
but they collected, one after the other,
all her disappointments & distresses.
Perhaps it was the crux of her story;
the carnage of belief. (That old construct.)
My folks fought their wars at home & away
praised the Father, the Son & the Holy Ghost.
My parents were such obedient pilgrims
they wedded for life, had too many children.

Married for life with too many children
then surprised by the birth of rock 'n' roll;
my parents shouldn't have relied on rhythm
or the discipline of a Catholic school.
Maybe it was the war our dad survived,
or Vietnam broadcast on TV screens.
Maybe it was just the backhand of God
that detached us kids from our parents' creed.
Vinyl LPs turned in my sisters' rooms
while cigarette smoke floated from their mouths.
Those were the days they were distant as moons
– teenaged, cool & unknowable.
They didn't want Mom's kind of redemption,
they had the Fab Four, their shaggy-haired saints.

The Fab Four, shaggy-haired saints of our youth
(& its requisite mix of drugs and beds)
like us, have been cherished, bereft & soothed.
In our brains there's a web – a complex thread,
of refurbished, disparate impressions
acquired & stored; encoded, retrieved;
the earworm, the recall, the confession.
Yeah, yeah, yeah, we danced & we were redeemed
but not even poetry will save our lives.
In that dream my mother touched my hand.
Too real. And I woke, longing –
Into all there is here, this Promised Land.
Our youth now just traces spun through our heads
& fifty percent of the Beatles are dead.

# Lament

When age collides with vanity
mammograms and blood tests;

when we are neither sunset, nor flower
nor brilliant season;

when our mothers are all departed
and when still, we are descended from Eve;

who will call us Darling?
Who will name us Sweetheart?

# Meltdown

I bought flower-printed leather oxfords the day before Chernobyl melted down.
I was in a shop near Montmartre, but far enough away that I never climbed that hill

instead I walked through the door under the sign *Chaussures*, enchanted –
ensorcelled! – by the prospect of a pair of pretty shoes from Paris.

I had within me then another girl, secret as clutter shoved into a drawer.
I was a tidy room decorated with heavy velour curtains and she,

the sacramental dark. My private fever starved by the Sunday liturgy.
So when Jesus held up the two fish and told the multitudes to eat I thought

he said: What you think is walleye is pickerel. Little fish, you are not
the walleye you want to be. So I pushed the soft meat down my gorge. Eat

or be eaten. April was still winter back home. A boy crashed his toboggan
when he failed to weave through the cluster of trees. His mother wept

for Jesus who had never lived through a northern winter like hers,
never lived through the high cost of soft-rayed freshwater fish. Anyway

during that nuclear catastrophe we were lost in serpentine streets
searching for the youth hostel with a kind madame whose name I don't recall.

We woke to the news and I tried not to think of the scissor and clank
from the gnathic mechanism of the future chewing up my time.

I tried not to think of the path to hell paved with
my new tainted shoes, my hidden self, my fevered dread.

## Drinking Alone on
## My Fifty-Fourth Birthday
## Or, My Dad and Disco Died
## Circa the Same Time

This bartender doesn't want to talk to me –

How would my dad win her over?
Would he joke until she laughed?
Put a cork in his ear?
Would he remind her of her granddad?
Would she know he was small-town famous?
Would he tip her like he was rich?
I will, I will tip the bartender like I am rich!

Before he died my dad and I danced at the CKOV Christmas party
& even though CKOV was turning country radio, we danced to Boney M.
It was weird disco-dancing with my dad & I was pretty wasted.

I miss the days of disco
& my brother, when he could talk any woman into his bed.
Reader, he lit their cigarettes!

The jazz in this bar is so cliché
it reminds me that being alive is so sad
& not to be depressing, but once we felt so important.

When he died in 1982, I thought my dad was old
I thought KC and the Sunshine Band were bullshit.

# When I Was Young I'd Listen to the Radio

I think about Karen Carpenter sometimes. Sometimes I think
about how good she seemed, how pure.

When I saw Karen Carpenter on TV, I saw myself. Myself, were I better,
had a smaller nose, was brunette, could sing like that and play the drums.

When Karen Carpenter died I didn't think of all my failed cucumber diets
I thought about the problem of the habit of obedience.

I thought how hard it is to kick the habit of obedience and how easy
to disappoint our mothers; how fat we look in our favourite dresses.

Richard M. Nixon was a fan, which, even before history, couldn't have helped
Karen's obsession with calories; couldn't have helped her desire to be more,
to be less.

Once, both Karen Carpenter and I were young; we had no idea that we were
beautiful. We had no idea that even our suffering could change.

Now, I turn her rich voice up loud –
It's taken me this whole life to recognize a good thing.

# Laws of Inheritance

The streets are full of the young and the young are so beautiful. The girls, a holy day of obligation. (It's part of their conversational charm to be drunk in the spirit.) And still, the future just keeps coming, as terrible as expected. Today you get up, you eat breakfast, you read the news, etc. Every day you get up, you eat breakfast, you read the news, etc. You always guessed it would end like this, every pundit; every theory of surmountable disease, cryonics and all of God's grim, worrying grace. Each decision brimming with consequences, and a terrific feeling of sinning.

That dream where I briefly became the world's fifth richest person
With plans to extend my days on earth to a span pinpointed as forever
Your eternal reminder that too much sun is beauty suicide

# The Beau Monde

1.

Mothers said, Now you know how it feels to be a woman, so
we slipped our sorrow down into our heels,
pushed our feet into pointy-toed shoes.

Daughters ate nothing; daughters ate everything,
daughters stuck their fingers down their throats.
Daughters started vegan lifestyle blogs.

After that daughters owed it all to their husbands
"His patience, his kindness, his relentless support."
Sometimes daughters owed it all to Jesus too.

Finally, mothers lay in their coffins, hands crossed over their hearts
fingernails painted pink-a-boo or imported bubbly or eternal optimist.

2.

A good narrative will always overwhelm data

Personal care, beauty and anti-aging
Healthy eating, nutrition and weight loss
Bridging the rift between luxury and the natural
The gender pain gap is only the tip of the iceberg
If you have the means you can be more about the package you come in
More about your abundance, more about your lucency

More about your biospiritual consciousness

3.

Don't think of Eve,
the most beautiful woman the world has ever known,
the first woman to be called wife,
the first mother to have a son who was a murderer and
the world's first dressmaker,
who begat Mary, who begat
the obedient daughter, who begat
the girl next door, who begat
the hippie, who begat
the yuppie, who begat
the video jockey, who begat
the blogess,
who is recovering from an eating disorder
after eating mixed green salads for sixteen years,
after having emergency surgery on her perforated septum,
not to mention the acid flashbacks
or the beating of her children with a wooden spoon
or her father's mean, mean idea of fashion.
Never think of Eve
the first and only woman born without sin.

4.

We brought it on ourselves,
by our insufficiency and by
the laws of attraction.
It wasn't our intention to become our mothers,
nevertheless, we too reached peak invisibility.
Our daughters, little magpies,
collected shiny apprehensions.

We said, Now you know how it feels to be a woman.

# Slip

In less time than you can imagine I was four years old; was I five? Suddenly I had yellow bell-bottom pants decked out with flowers & a baby doll to call my own; I called her Baby. My father was very tall with hands the size of entire episodes of *Hockey Night in Canada* & I held his hand on that last day of his life, he was dying hard but from the far reaches of his effort he held my hand too, or he didn't. Whatever, there was no pulling him back.

I think there must be so many kinds of loneliness. I remember my parents drove theirs in a Dodge Polara. Later my mom drove a green Ford Galaxie station wagon that my brother once jacked, then her luscious peach Cougar, then a long-nosed Chrysler LeBaron. After that, she could no longer draw a clock.

But first, I was fourteen. Donna Summer was the undisputed queen of disco. I drank apricot wine we found fermenting in a basement. The streets bloomed under that buzz but I was unfit for teenaged boys with their sun-bleached hair. I was unfit for their confidence & their impatience to feel up girls in the bushes by Sarsons Beach. The world was their waterbed.

Near the end of his life my father rolled out of his waterbed and snapped his brittle collarbone. Before that my grandmother wore black, broad-heeled oxfords. Loneliness can travel for generations in a pair of commonsense shoes.

# A Thing on Beauty

Think of collagen as scaffolding for your face
& every time you consume sugar you remove a piece of that scaffolding
& as collagen breaks down and becomes destroyed, wrinkles begin to appear
& you are left without the qualities that are typical of beauty.

As you consume sugar the scaffolding of your good looks crumbles
then the messy state of your soul becomes writ bold across your face.
You, now without the qualities that are typical of beauty,
find your individual unit of capital is no longer in demand.

The messy state of your soul is written boldly across your face;
you crave too often & you are devoted to eating.
Your individual unit of capital is no longer in demand
& women have been burned for less than that hair on your chin.

You surrender to craving too often plus you are devoted to eating,
your collagen is being destroyed and the wrinkles, the wrinkles!
Women have been burned for less than that hair on your chin (& other stories).
Try not to think of collagen, the scaffolding for your face.

## For As You Were

We are a complicated list of systems that give rise to Being,
childhood embedded in the involuntary motion of the cardiac muscle.
The narrative of our damages a galloping horse.
The litany of our litanies. Our Fathers,
our brothers and sisters, amen.
Our mothers at the beginning of very good.
And all those names that broke our bones.
Oh, skinnamarinky dinky dink, you lovers,

cast off the tyrannical minutes ticking at your wrists,
and the slackening skin, and the worsening feet.
To think youth led you to this place of mercy,
where now you dwell in promise and, that old saw, the heart,
where everything, starting again, shakes you open
and the tender adolescent rises in your touch.

## Talking Head

Once I was the source, all fountain, all legs –
Gone now the joy of lighting myself on fire
of running headlong into calamity.
My kingdom for a pair of comfortable heels!
My body, as ever, the enemy,
ill-fated as the socialist project
in the parliament of greed.
Still, each year the birds get drunk on summer.
And, like us, we who invented love,
(us bipeds with our roaring cunts
us idiots of desire, us fat drunks)
the birds, beloved of the trees, return
as we must also return to what we've lost
to our mums, to our bodies & to the earth.

# Pentimento

Another day and the dog & cat are sleeping in the warmth of the fire
I think the SAD lamp could try harder
I should never have let the habit of sugar develop
in myself, in my children. Oh, the potato chips!
Such pimples! such eczema! such sensitive skins.

We are alive in the living body of mobile technology
We can eat all the fried chicken we desire!

It's just another ordinary day. If I put on mascara
I will have to wash it off. I think that lamp does a poor imitation
of the sun. Now my children have lovers and bad habits.
I have the glycemic index and shame. And billions of fat cells.
All of us created in some likeness of –

The Eucharist:
Those quiet mornings
my brother placed the marshmallow on my tongue,
Body of Christ, he intoned.
He is still a preacher
& I still seek the gesture of elevation,
the transubstantiation of sugar to Glory
in this accident of substance I call my body

now waiting for a band of pink to burn
off this morning's lavender cloud.
Sidewalks are dotted with ice patches
snowbanks clot the roads
& the light casts its gilt patina on the stones of St John's,
like if God were a cinematographer
like if I believed in God.

I'm thinking of my adolescent season
when everything made me weep,
when crying was a gesture not a feeling.

So, how's this for symbolism?
The dog and I were walking toward the crow
& the crow was pecking at some frozen vomit
but first the crow was strutting toward her bounty
& I was thinking, look at that crow strutting on the sidewalk.
I was thinking don't screw with that crow
that crow would be happy to mess my dog up.
For a second I wondered what the symbolism of the crow might be
& then I thought the symbolism of the crow was unimportant –
It was the crow who was important,
pecking at the drunkard's excess,
& now it belongs to the crow
who, once slighted, will never forget.

I was a child afraid of the land, all that vast frozen,
I was afraid of boys & their tongues & steep toboggan hills,
I was afraid of going too fast, of being swallowed by the snow.
I was a child who was afraid I was going to hell, obviously
I was a child who was afraid of dying in a sledding accident
on a treed hillside, where anyway, I'd already been chosen for the ugly boy
not surprisingly as I was the ugly girl; I was the girl who talked too much.
I had no mystery, my teeth were crooked & I had no tits.
I thought I'd never get my period, my truest bloody friend
those Saturday nights when I lied & said I had a babysitting job.

Well anyway, I repent nothing –

A lumpish organ flutters in my chest, poor little fist trying to avoid cliché

I know I am a sinner

I'm churlish & desolate

but drawn beneath our ordinary days is that wretched coffee

& our first kisses standing outside your car before your long drive home.

# Lament

The day opens its gaping mouth

(It is as reasonable to ask *why not* as it is to ask *why*.
My father said that and he is dead now thirty-three years,
my oldest brother nearly nine, my mother eight, my former partner ten
and my sister's son just three years.
But you could just as well say for all eternity.)

the leaves vibrate, bracing for their abscission.

We are so tiny.

# Keynesian Economics

After the war they
sent enough of our dads home
to pay the rent &
to buy Country Squire wagons.
It was the golden age of capitalism

after the war
& our dads taught us all how
to hold our liquor;
they gave enough of our dads
work for that, after the war.

# God Almighty, Now You're Just Morose

Our mother is dead
She suffered as much as she'd ever suffered
cognitive deterioration was all the rage
You had to get there on a riverboat

Our mother is dead
Her city was smaller & then she was a girl suddenly
her daddy was dearly departed
Not a muscle in her bananas face moved

Our mother is dead
After the Great Depression she was admired
by soldiers at dances & then by the sailor
Little Mary Hickey liked to cut a rug

It was her war too, darling –

# Happy Days

As a pseudo-orphan in Peace Country
During the summer of love I saved
My brothers' lives that day at the frog pond
Calling, Come back in or Mom will kill you!

We had our idylls on the Beatton's banks
Which curves across the boreal forest
And muskeg and rises at Pink Mountain,
The so-called Serengeti of the north.

Before the overwhelming present came
The overwhelming past, the discipline,
The un-naming, the ancestral homeland,

The Alaska Highway where the buffalo roam,
Or so they say. Boreal diversity
Reduced and formed by fire, like all cool kids.

# The Food Our Mothers Made

We ate their hard little roasts

Their hamburger surprises

In the fall we crept into orchards and stole apples from the trees

We ate only cucumber for a week

We were never skinny enough

We chewed grape Hubba Bubba

It seemed impossible we would live so long

Become this old, this fat

It was the 1970s

Maybe we'd become movie stars

Or disco queens

Or millionaires

Oh, the smoothness of our skin

We drank gin and pink lemonade

We drank vodka and orange juice

We floated across the roads in a father's cream-coloured Cadillac DeVille

We told our mothers we were at sleepovers

Look at us in our tight jeans and high-heeled boots

Little deities of the suburb

Monstrous in our appetites

It was the time of our lives

Before we became insurance brokers

Or single moms

Or sober

# Rules of Golf

The guys are on the course for first tee time; the gals are at home, annoyed by annoying children. There will be no help until after lunch and it's their vacation too.

No shirts, no shoes, no service and no sugary cereal.

The sons-in-law will have consumed alcohol with the father; the daughters will be at the beach with the mother (the hateful sand, the dull sun) and the children who, this close to the water, must be watched at all times.

The tennis courts are Out of Bounds, the parking lot is Out of Bounds; teenaged superciliousness is Out of Bounds.

There will be long silences
The unmarried daughter will bring wine
(who are we kidding? everybody brings booze)
There will be barbecued burgers and potato salad
There will be cherries

In 5.5 years father will be dead and one son-in-law will have been replaced. At or around the funeral someone will say our father who art in heaven and all the children will laugh

# Consolation

Why do we read our poems aloud like this,

when we would never say
to our lovers: I hate you
and the history of harm you bring to our bed
like this?

♩ ♭

We would never ask our dying mother for the key to her apartment,
not, like this,

♩ ♭

and we would never say: Tonight

♩ ♩

I will eat the leftover Chinese food and maybe some meatballs.

♩ ♩ ♭ ♩ ♩ ♫♩ ♭ ♭ ♩ ♫ ♩ ♩ ♩

Even though it's true, all we think of is food
(and maybe, sometimes, fucking) even in the midst of death,
when we eat tiny triangle sandwiches on department store bread.

And we do not say: Thank you for coming,
to the last living friend of our mother's youth
who holds herself up now on a metal walker, and who wept
so fiercely for all those girls who have shed *the heartache*
*and the thousand natural shocks that flesh is heir to*[5]
like this.

And we do not take her papery hand in ours
because even more terrible than our mother's frantic end
is the last living friend of her youth,
proof that there is no consolation in time.

---

5    William Shakespeare, *Hamlet.*

# Heavenly Body

My mother's third baby died at ten days. The nun said, Get back
on the saddle and voila, here is our sister!
Oh, her legendary baby-pink satin pantsuit, her green eyes
her sexual revolution and mine (if that's how it could be described).
In retrospect, perhaps I should have fucked more people
if only I'd understood where time would lead me
its creeping, petty pace:
Disaster, disaster, hyperbole, bath time
crack pipe, marriage, crack pipe, sweet pea –

What's bigger, what's more unframed, what's further
than ten thousand years, except the universe of our self?
Consider the estimated 100 trillion cells of the adult human body
and its colonies of roughly 300 trillion commensal bacteria.
Still, I am crying for no obvious reason (or maybe for my mother)
and, of course, it's November when I'm always at my lowest
not to mention the persistence of trauma in the microbiome of my gut
and its deep link to my central nervous system
and my Catholic leaning toward confession
and my mother and her third baby, Terrance.

First she lost a son then she gained a daughter and a daughter
and a son and a son and a daughter; proof of my mother's stamina.
Like my mother I pollute myself with sugar, mistreat
my bacterial collaborators; dwell on past sins.
I refill a tablespoon with maple syrup and swallow the sweet
remedy.
Sweet as my sister's baby-pink satin pantsuit,
the one I was always too fat to wear
like my mother and her fear and her anxious warnings.

# Dad in Rockyview ICU 1981;
# Notes After Tracheotomy

Another great supper – T-bone in nose
Suction, pee & radio, in that order
In my position you would try reading anything
I'm bored
I've read everything and I'm going nuts
What took you so f'ing long today?
Nothing has been so overestimated as sex & so underestimated as a good pee

For Christ's sake – I don't want to sleep – just talk & I'll listen
I'm not tired
I've been scared before
I spent 5 years overseas in Navy in WW2

Besides I like the ambulance rides
Those "red light" taxis don't come cheap either
I had a hell of an ambulance ride yesterday – lights, bells, sirens
We went through construction areas like shit through a goose
But I'd like to go home soon

When I get out I want some new jeans & "penny type" loafers besides
a good warm coat – maybe shearling?
& no bitching about cost

Guy in bed next to me died last night – I didn't sleep too well – just a young guy
I'm a bit down but I guess you can't be up all the time
The body shrinks, the teeth don't

It's a great view
Pissy-assed lake, some flat prairie & some big fucking rocky hills

For supper I'll have 1 filet mignon, fried mushrooms,
medium baked spud with sour cream, butter, chives and bacon bits
If I can't have that, then another 2 cans of that shit.


Pain in the heart – I'm in love with my nurses

# Lament

My father has been dead for so long now
soon I will be old
Who will remember my mother
her moods
her sugar addiction
her Rothmans
& her peach-coloured 1977 Mercury Cougar
that we sailed into the ditch that Sunday morning before Mass
when my father's death was so sharp and everything was over

That Sunday I learned to turn into a skid I learned not to brake
when my mother said, I should have turned into the skid
(I like to think my mother said that
but it was in her nature to panic and slam her foot on the brake
my mother was simply relieved to not have caused more damage, to drive out
of the ditch and into the parking lot of St. Charles Garnier Catholic Church)
In that way my mother was heroic
And oh her manifest virtues
Loyalty
Stubbornness
Anger
Silence
A prudent use of pharmaceuticals

It is a sin to complain
my mother would be the first to say so
but there is still so much I want to know
and my mother is dead
Soon I will be old

# The History of Exploration

My mother was ironing the sheets,
blue ironing board, wicker basket;
the drapes were drawn
and it was boring, boring in that room.
I don't know where my brothers were.

Or, I'm confusing this with Bobby Kennedy's murder
and the Technicolor news flashing in black & white
on the TV screen in Peace Country.
But for sure my mother stood by the hot iron,
and the sheets had been on the line,
and the Armstrong boy held his hand to his face.

I didn't see the lunar module, or the man,
I saw my mother in the long shadow
of laundry and ground beef.
Pay attention, she said. History is in the making,
while the heirs of Felipa Columbus, with
their freshly coiffed hair, made do with *gobs of coffee*.
Joan Aldrin, cigarette in hand, turned away from the TV.
The stars had warned against throwing caution to the wind.
My mother folded each white sheet into a square,
stirred powdered milk and sugar into her Sanka
and held a match to the tip of her Rothmans.

In forty years it would all be forgotten,
the white sheets, the landing, the cheerful wives and anxious children.
But the cliché moon, diminished by electric street lights
continued its ordinary orbit and my mother cried out,
Sweet Jesus, to no one in particular.

# Upon Hearing of Another Celebrity Death by Cancer

The truth is I think of my own father
dead at fifty-nine, I think of myself
fatherless; my dad dying and dying
I think: I hope that's not cancer, that _____
My whole life my dad has been vanishing,
lost (*sing it*) to the great by and by –
I exaggerate; there were those fourteen
years when I was a girl & Dad was well.
Plus there were the forty years before then
nearly impossible to imagine.
The thought of it, my father as a child,
his parents as strange to him as mine to me.
My dad got into the war & fist fights,
afterwards he got into more whisky
then my dad got into sports radio.
He was at the top of his game when he died.

My father, a minor celebrity
himself, packed the house at his funeral Mass.

# Embodied

On the way to our rental cottage I see K in the parking lot of our town's charming bakery & gourmet food shop. After we greet one another, from the deep recesses of my psyche, my father tells her, "H is inside buying sausageshits."

Then K tells me she left J at home to do the linens like a weird 1950s throwback. "It relaxes her," K says. She doesn't even notice my dad.

These days my father is one long occupying dad joke, perhaps it is my age, so close now to his final age, to the last time we talked, to his demanding pain. And why does my friend J iron her sheets? I think it's safe to blame the mother.

Later, on the return half of my long swim with H, I look toward the beckoning dock, and – door to this thin place opened by the swimming noodle tucked securely under my arms – my mom takes my physical form and quips, "It's a long way to Tipperary."

Sometimes my mom just starts singing "Make the World Go Away," although she only remembers the first two lines, and we never need a thin place for her to pop up with that little number. I have my mother's legs, and my mother's belly, and her high school grad photo tattooed on my arm.

They're such good parents, my mom and dad –
Always returning to meet my grief, and still insisting,
If I'm going to live in their house it's going to be by their rules

# *Pastoral, 2020*

We are past the hum of the city and silence hangs
No, not silence –
There is the chorus of spring peepers, chirping,
& the dog straining against her leash,
all she wants is to snap the neck of a squirrel.
Beech leaves hang from thin branches like paper lanterns.
We are walking on a carpet of last year's weathered leaves.
The puppy bounds up and down moss-covered limestone walls.
A blue jay creaks
& then the cry of a loon,
geese, sparrows, robins;
iconic, right?
It's almost enough to shake off the dread
that pulls me out of each night's sleep
my children are locked in their city
I am here, locked in mine
& we are waiting.
We do and we don't know what we are waiting for

# *Evensong*

– on the other hand, we're still alive &
lilacs, behind the elm, are uncurling.
Across the street, Buddhist prayer flags snap
in the wind; two monks climb out of a car.
Everything we are in these shifting forms
calls for a resumption of fucking.
It's a cliché to say youth is fleeting,
(those years when we were led by our bodies
from one devastation to the next lover)
yet here we are, aged & unsightly,
in our metaphorical Augusts, all
the fragrant dung & steam of spring departed.
The monks move slowly into the temple
& our hands, our mouths, rise in exaltation.

# ACKNOWLEDGEMENTS

I am grateful to be living as a settler in the traditional territories of the Haudenosaunee Confederacy and the Anishinabek Nation on lands that are included in the Dish with One Spoon Wampum Belt Covenant.

The following poems were previously published. Many thanks to the editors who selected my work to be included in their publications.

"TBH" in *The Puritan* 38 and in *Best Canadian Poetry 2018*

"Humans on Mars" in *Room Magazine* 40, no. 4

"Current Mood" (section one) in *Arc Poetry* 83

"Consolation" in *Poetry Is Dead* 19

"Upon Hearing of Another Celebrity Death by Cancer"
    in *Another Dysfunctional Cancer Poem Anthology*

"Happy Days" by Toronto Poetry Vendors

"They Will Take My Island" was published online at
    theywilltakemyisland.blogspot.com

"The History of Exploration" in *Grain Magazine* 45, no. 1

"The History of Exploration" was developed during a project initiated and supported by the Liaison of Independent Filmmakers of Toronto. I was paired with the artist Nurielle Stern to develop the video *Scraps*. *Scraps* was screened August 19–21 as a part of Labspace Studio's (re)collection project. If you're interested, the video can be viewed at Nurielle Stern's website www.deepbreathely.com.

Language From Bloomberg.com, "Goop Is Making a Killing off Women Who Want More Than a Doctor's Advice," Riley Griffin, March 18, 2019, is used in "Le Beau Monde" #2.

I'm very thankful for the financial support this collection received from the Canada Council for the Arts Grants to Professional Writers program, as well as the Ontario Arts Council's Writers' Reserve Program.

In the spring of 2017 I spent two weeks living and writing in Calgary in Loft 112's studio apartment. Thank you to Lisa Murphy-Lamb for this terrific opportunity and to Sharon Stevens for hooking us up.

I have so much gratitude for the Villanelles, Ashley, Kirsteen, Sadiqa, Sarah, Susan and Ying. Your astute critiques have improved my work greatly and your friendship feels like home. What a joy it is to dial in and find your brilliant selves online. *hands praying emoji on repeat*

Thank you, Paul Vermeersch, Noelle Allen, Ashley Hisson and the Wolsak and Wynn team. It is a pleasure to work with you all again. And thank you to Kilby Smith-McGregor for the brilliant cover design.

It's been a tough couple of years. I'm grateful that my kids continue to send texts and share TikTok videos, and that my Kingston bubble shares meals and dog walks. But mostly I am thankful to be sharing this life with Helen, whose presence makes everything better.

**NANCY JO CULLEN**'s poetry and fiction have appeared in *The Puritan*, *Grain*, *filling Station*, *Plenitude*, *Prairie Fire*, *Arc*, *This Magazine*, *Best Canadian Poetry 2018*, *Room*, *The Journey Prize* and *Best Canadian Fiction 2012*. Nancy is the 2010 recipient for the Dayne Ogilvie Prize for LGBTQ+ Emerging Writers. She's published three collections of poetry with Frontenac House and a collection of short stories, *Canary*, with Biblioasis. Her first novel, *The Western Alienation Merit Badge*, was shortlisted for the 2020 Amazon Canada First Novel Award.